AF258496

THIS JOURNAL BELONGS TO

Date

Date

Date ___________

Date

Date

Date _______________

Date

Date

Date

Date

Date ______________

Date

Date

Date

Date

Date

Date

Date ______________________

Date

Date

Date _______________

Date

Date

Date _______________________

Date

Date ________________________

Date _______________________

Date

Date

Date ______________

Date

Date

Date _______________

Date

Date

Date ___________

Date

Date

Date _______________________

Date

Date

Date ________________

Date

Date ______________________

Date ___________________

Date

Date

Date

Date

Date ______________

Date

Date

Date

Date

Date _______________________

Date _______________

Date _______________

Date

Date

Date

Date _______________

Date

Date ______________________

Date

Date

Date

Date ______________________

Date

Date

Date _______________________

Date _______________

Date ______________

Date ___________

Date

Date

Date

Date

Date ___________________

Date ______________________

Date _______________________

Date

Date 

Date

Date ___________

Date ________________

Date ___________

Date

Date _______________

Date

Date ___________

Date

Date ___________________

Date

Date _______________

Date

Date ____________________

Date

Date

Date ___________________________

Date ____

Date

Date _______________

Date

Date

Date

Date

Date

Date

Date ___________

Date

Date

Date _______________________

Date

Date

Date

Date _______________

Date ________________

Date ________________

Date

Date ____________________

Date _______________________

Date ________________

Date _______________

Date _______________________

Date

Date

Date

Date ___________________

Date _______________

Date ___________________________

Date

Date ___________________

Date

Date _______________

Date

Date

Date

Date

Date

Date

Date

Date

Date ________________

Date

Date

Thank you.

We hope you enjoyed our journal.

As a small family company, your feedback is very important to us.

Please let us know how you like our journal at:

mollymcluke@gmail.com